ENCOURAGEMENT FROM
90
MINUTES IN
HEAVEN

ENCOURAGEMENT FROM

90

MINUTES IN
HEAVEN

Selections from the Life-Changing *New York Times* Bestseller

DON PIPER

with CECIL MURPHEY

Revell

a division of Baker Publishing Group
Grand Rapids, Michigan

© 2004, 2008, 2011 by Don Piper

Published by Revell
a division of Baker Publishing Group
P.O. Box 6287, Grand Rapids, MI 49516-6287
www.revellbooks.com

Revised edition of *90 Minutes in Heaven: An Inspiring Story of Life beyond Death*,
published 2008

Printed in the United States of America

Library of Congress Cataloging-in-Publication Data

Piper, Don, 1950–
    Encouragement from 90 minutes in heaven : selections from the life-changing New York Times bestseller / Don Piper with Cecil Murphey.
        p.   cm.
    Rev. ed. of: 90 minutes in heaven.
    Includes bibliographical references (p.   ).
    ISBN 978-0-8007-3451-0 (pbk.)
    1. Piper, Don, 1950–. 2. Heaven—Christianity. 3. Near-death experiences—Religious aspects—Christianity. I. Murphey, Cecil. II. Piper, Don, 1950– 90 minutes in heaven. III. Title.
BT846.3.P562 2010
231.7′3092—dc22   2010033519

Unless otherwise indicated, Scripture is taken from the *Holy Bible*, New Living Translation, copyright © 1996. Used by permission of Tyndale House Publishers, Inc., Wheaton, Illinois 60189. All rights reserved.

Scripture marked GW is taken from GOD'S WORD®. Copyright 1995 by God's Word to the Nations. All rights reserved.

Scripture marked NIV is taken from the Holy Bible, New International Version®, NIV®. Copyright © 1973, 1978, 1984 by Biblica, Inc.™ Used by permission of Zondervan. All rights reserved worldwide. www.zondervan.com

To protect the privacy of those who have shared their stories with the author, some details and names have been changed.

11 12 13 14 15 16 17   7 6 5 4

Contents

Prologue

When *90 Minutes in Heaven* was first published in 2004, I had no idea how people would respond. But in the years since then, as I've traveled in the United States and abroad, I've been amazed at the ways my experience has touched so many individuals.

If you read *90 Minutes in Heaven* you know I began that book by saying I wrote

7

it in self-defense. By that, I meant I wrote it so I would personally never have to tell the story again. I must confess I have failed in that objective completely. Since its 2004 release I have traveled all over this world and spoken to millions in person, on the radio, on TV, and in other books.

Indeed, what did happen after *90 Minutes* was published has become an international phenomenon, with editions in every format possible—including some that didn't exist when the original book hit bookstores. Now in forty languages and with nearly five million copies in print, *90 Minutes in Heaven* has brought hope, encouragement, and inspiration to millions worldwide.

That's what led us to release a new edition of this riveting testimony. In this small book, you'll read the story of what happened to me when I died. You'll also read just a few of the stories that others have shared with me. Some have graciously given permission to use their names. On other stories, I've carefully changed the details to preserve privacy.

I also wanted to share with you some of my favorite Scriptures and quotations about heaven, comfort, and prayer. I trust they'll be as meaningful to you as they are to me. Dwight Moody said, "Heaven is a prepared place for a prepared people." I've made my reservation, and I know I'll be going back someday. Prayerfully, I'll see you there, too.

1

The Accident

That is why we can say with
confidence,
"The Lord is my helper,
    so I will not be afraid.
    What can mere mortals do
        to me?"

Hebrews 13:6

The Baptist General Convention of Texas (BGCT) holds annual statewide conferences. In January 1989, they chose the north shore of Lake Livingston where the Union Baptist Association, composed of all Baptist churches in the greater Houston area, operates a large conference center called Trinity Pines. The conference focused on church growth, and I went because I was seriously considering starting a new church.

The conference started on Monday and was scheduled to end with lunch on

Wednesday. On Tuesday night, I joined a BGCT executive and friend named J. V. Thomas for a long walk. J. V. had become a walker after his heart attack, so we exercised together the last night of the conference.

Months earlier, I had begun thinking that it was time for me to start a new congregation. Before embarking on such a venture, I wanted as much information as I could get. I knew that J. V. had as much experience and knowledge about new church development as anyone in the

Despite the cold, rainy weather, we had a wonderful time together. . . . It would be the last time I would ever walk normally.

14

BGCT. Because he had started many successful churches in the state, most of us recognized him as the expert. As we walked together that night, we talked about my starting a new church, when to do it, and where to plant it. I wanted to know the hardships as well as the pitfalls to avoid. He answered my seemingly endless questions and raised issues I hadn't thought about.

We walked and talked for about an hour. Despite the cold, rainy weather, we had a wonderful time together. J. V. remembers that time well.

So do I, but for a different reason: It would be the last time I would ever walk normally.

On Wednesday morning the weather worsened. A steady rain fell. Had the temperature been only a few degrees colder, we couldn't have traveled, because everything would have been frozen.

The morning meetings started on time. The final speaker did something Baptist preachers almost never do—he finished early. Instead of lunch, the staff at Trinity Pines served us brunch at about ten thirty. I had packed the night before, so everything was stowed in my red 1986 Ford Escort.

As soon as we finished brunch, I said good-bye to all my friends and got into my car to drive back to the church where I was on staff, South Park Baptist Church in Alvin, a Houston bedroom community.

When I started the engine, I remembered that only three weeks earlier I had received a traffic ticket for not wearing a seat belt. I had been on my way to preach for a pastor friend who was going to have throat surgery. A Texas trooper had caught me. That ticket still lay on the passenger seat, reminding me to pay it as soon as I returned to Alvin. Until I received the ticket, I had not usually worn a seat belt, but after that I changed my ways.

> *I carefully fastened my seat belt. That small act would be a crucial decision.*

When I looked at that ticket, I thought, *I don't want to be stopped again.* So I carefully fastened my seat belt. That small act would be a crucial decision.

There were two ways to get back to Houston and on to Alvin. As soon as I reached the gates of Trinity Pines, I had to choose either to drive through Livingston and down Highway 59 or to head west to Huntsville and hit I-45, often called the Gulf Freeway. Each choice is probably about the same distance. Every other time to and from Trinity Pines I had driven Highway 59. That morning I decided to take the Gulf Freeway.

I was relieved that we had been able to leave early. It was only a few minutes after 11:00, so I could get back to the church by 2:00. The senior minister had led a group to the Holy Land and left me responsible for

Before they call, I will

answer.

While they're still

speaking, I will hear.

Isaiah 65:24 GW

our midweek service at South Park Church.
He had also asked me to preach for the
next two Sundays. That night was a prayer
meeting, which required little preparation,
but I needed to work on my sermon for the
following Sunday morning.

Before I left Alvin, I had written a draft
for the first sermon titled "I Believe in a
Great God." As I drove, I planned to glance
over the sermon and evaluate what I had
written so far.

Many times since then I've thought
about my decision to take the Gulf Freeway.
It's amazing how we pay no attention to
simple decisions at the time they're made.
Yet I would remind myself that even the
smallest decisions often hold significant

consequences. This was one of those choices.

I pulled out of Trinity Pines, turned right, and headed down Texas Highway 19. That would take me to Huntsville and intersect with I-45, leading to Houston. I didn't have to drive far before I reached Lake Livingston, a man-made lake, created by damming the Trinity River. What was once a riverbed is now a large, beautiful lake. Spanning Lake Livingston is a two-lane highway whose roadbed has been built up above the level of the lake. The road has no shoulders, making it extremely narrow. I would have to drive across a long expanse of water on that narrow road until I reached the other side. I had no premonitions about the trip, although I was aware of the road's lack of shoulders.

At the end of the highway across the lake is the original bridge over the Trinity River. Immediately after the bridge, the road rises sharply, climbing the bluff above the Trinity's riverbed. This sharp upturn makes visibility a problem for drivers in both directions.

It was a dangerous bridge, and as I would learn later, several accidents had occurred on it.

This was my first time to see the bridge, and it looked curiously out of place. I have no idea of the span, but the bridge is quite long. It's an old bridge with a massive, rusty steel superstructure. Other than the immediate road ahead, I could see little, and I certainly didn't glimpse any other traffic. It was a dangerous bridge, and as I would learn later, several accidents had occurred on it. (Although no longer used, the bridge is still there. The state built another one beside it.)

I drove at about fifty miles an hour because it was, for me, uncharted territory. I braced my shoulders against the chill inside the car. The wind made the morning seem even colder than it was. The steady rain had turned into a cloudburst. I would be happy to finally reach Alvin again. About 11:45 A.M., just before I cleared the east end of the bridge, an eighteen-wheeler driven by an inmate, a trustee at the Texas Department of Corrections, weaved across

Never stop praying.

Whatever happens,

give thanks, because it

is God's will in Christ

Jesus that you do this.

*1 Thessalonians
5:17–18 GW*

the center line and hit my car head-on. The truck sandwiched my small car between the bridge railing and the driver's side of the truck. All those wheels went right on top of my car and smashed it.

I remember parts of the accident, but most of my information came from the accident report and people at the scene.

From the description I've received from witnesses, the truck then veered off to the other side of the narrow bridge and sideswiped two other cars. They were in front of the truck and had already passed me going in the opposite direction. The police record says that the truck was driving fast—at least sixty miles an hour—when it struck my car. The inexperienced driver finally brought the truck to a stop almost at the end of the bridge.

A young Vietnamese man was in one vehicle that was hit, and an elderly Caucasian man was in the other. Although shaken up, both drivers suffered only minor cuts and bruises. They refused help, so the paramedics transported neither man to the hospital.

Because of the truck's speed, the accident report states that the impact was about 110 miles an hour. That is, the truck struck me while going sixty miles an hour, and I was carefully cruising along at fifty. The inmate received a citation for failure to control his vehicle and speeding. Information later came out that the inmate wasn't licensed to drive the truck. At the prison, supervisors had asked for volunteers to drive their truck to pick up food items and bring them back. Because he was the only volunteer, they let him drive their supply truck. Two guards followed close behind him in another state-owned pickup.

After the accident, the truck driver didn't have a scratch on him. The prison truck received little damage. However, the heavy vehicle had crushed my Ford and pushed it from the narrow road. Only the bridge railing stopped my car from going into the lake.

According to those who were at the scene, the guards called for medical backup from the prison, and they arrived a few minutes later. Someone examined me, found no pulse, and declared that I had been killed instantly.

I have no recollection of the impact or anything that happened afterward.

In one powerful, overwhelming second, I died.

2

My Time in Heaven

He was afraid and said, "How awesome is this place! This is none
other than the house of God; this is
the gate of heaven."

Genesis 28:17 NIV

When I died, I didn't flow through a long, dark tunnel. I had no sense of fading away or of coming back. I never felt my body being transported into the light. I heard no voices calling to me or anything else. Simultaneous with my last recollection of seeing the bridge and the rain, a light enveloped me, with a brilliance beyond earthly comprehension or description. Only that.

In my next moment of awareness, I was standing in heaven.

⸺⸻⸺

Joy pulsated through me as I looked around, and at that moment I became aware of a large crowd of people. They stood in front of a brilliant, ornate gate. I have no idea how far away they were; such things as distance didn't matter. As the crowd rushed toward me, I didn't see Jesus, but I did see people I had known. As they surged toward me, I knew instantly that all of them had died during my lifetime. Their presence seemed absolutely natural.

They rushed toward me, and every person was smiling, shouting, and praising God. Although no one said so, intuitively I knew they were my celestial welcoming committee. It was as if they had all gathered just outside heaven's gate, waiting for me.

The first person I recognized was Joe Kulbeth, my grandfather. He looked exactly as I remembered him, with his shock of white hair and what I called a big banana nose. He stopped momentarily and stood in front of me. A grin covered his face. I may have called his name, but I'm not sure.

They rushed toward me, and every person was smiling, shouting, and praising God. Although no one said so, intuitively I knew they were my celestial welcoming committee.

"Donnie!" (That's what my grandfather always called me.) His eyes lit up, and he held out

33

his arms as he took the last steps toward me. He embraced me, holding me tightly. He was once again the robust, strong grandfather I had remembered as a child.

I'd been with him when he suffered a heart attack at home and had ridden with him in the ambulance. I had been standing just outside the emergency room at the hospital when the doctor walked out and faced me. He shook his head and said softly, "We did everything we could."

My grandfather released me, and as I stared into his face, an ecstatic bliss overwhelmed me. I didn't think about his heart attack or his death, because I couldn't get past the joy of our reunion. How either of us reached heaven seemed irrelevant.

I have no idea why my grandfather was the first person I saw. Perhaps it had something to do with my being there when he died. He wasn't one of the great spiritual guides of my life, although he certainly influenced me positively in that way.

After being hugged by my grandfather, I don't remember who was second or third. The crowd surrounded me. Some hugged me and a few kissed my cheek, while others pumped my hand. Never had I felt more loved.

One person in that greeting committee was Mike Wood, my childhood friend. Mike was special because he invited me to Sunday school and was influential in my becoming a Christian. Mike was the most devoted young Christian I knew. He was

also a popular kid and had lettered four
years in football, basketball, and track and
field, an amazing feat. He also became a
hero to me, because he lived the Christian
lifestyle he often talked about. After high
school, Mike received a full scholarship to
Louisiana State University. When he was
nineteen, Mike was killed in a car wreck.
It broke my heart when I heard about his
death, and it took me a long time to get
over it. His death was the biggest shock and
most painful experience I'd had up to that
time in my life.

When I attended his funeral, I wondered
if I would ever stop crying. I couldn't
understand why God had taken such a
dedicated disciple. Through the years since
then, I had never been able to forget the

36

pain and sense of loss. Not that I thought of him all the time, but when I did, sadness came over me.

Now I saw Mike in heaven. As he slipped his arm around my shoulder, my pain and grief vanished. Never had I seen Mike smile so brightly. I still didn't know why, but the joyousness of the place wiped away any questions. Everything felt blissful. Perfect.

When he was nineteen, Mike was killed in a car wreck.... His death was the biggest shock and most painful experience I'd had up to that time in my life.

More and more people reached for me and called me by name. I felt overwhelmed by the number

37

Has the world been so

kind that you should

leave the world with

regret? There are better

things ahead than any

we leave behind.

C. S. Lewis

of people who had come to welcome me to heaven. There were so many of them, and I had never imagined anyone being as happy as they all were. Their faces radiated a serenity I had never seen on earth. All were full of life and expressed radiant joy.

Time had no meaning. However, for clarity, I'll relate this experience in terms that refer to time.

I saw my great-grandfather, heard his voice, and felt his embrace as he told me how excited he was that I had come to join them. I saw Barry Wilson, who had been my classmate in high school but later drowned in a lake. Barry hugged me, and his smile radiated a happiness I didn't know was possible. He and everyone who followed praised God and told me how excited they were to see me and to welcome me to heaven and to the fellowship they enjoyed.

Just then, I spotted two teachers who had loved me and often talked to me about Jesus Christ. As I walked among them, I became aware of the wide variety of ages—old and young and every age in between. Many of them hadn't known each other on earth, but each had influenced my life in some way. Even though they hadn't met on earth, they seemed to know each other now.

As I try to explain this, my words seem weak and hardly adequate, because I have to

Just then, I spotted two teachers who had loved me and often talked to me about Jesus Christ.

use earthly terms to refer to unimaginable joy, excitement, warmth, and total happiness. Everyone continually embraced me, touched me, spoke to me, laughed, and praised God. This seemed to go on for a long time, but I didn't tire of it.

My father is one of eleven children. Some of his brothers and sisters had as many as thirteen children. When I was a kid, our family reunions were so huge we rented an entire city park in Monticello, Arkansas. We Pipers are affectionate, with a lot of hugging and kissing whenever we come together. None of those earthly family reunions, however, prepared me for the sublime gathering of saints I experienced at the gates of heaven.

Those who had gathered at Monticello were some of the same people waiting for me at the gates of heaven. Heaven was many things, but without a doubt, it was the greatest family reunion of all.

Everything I experienced was like a first-class buffet for the senses. I had never felt such powerful embraces or feasted my eyes on such beauty. Heaven's light and texture defy earthly eyes or explanation. Warm, radiant light engulfed me. As I looked around, I could hardly grasp the vivid, dazzling colors. Every hue and tone surpassed anything I had ever seen.

With all the heightened awareness of my senses, I felt as if I had never seen, heard, or felt anything so real before. I don't recall that I tasted anything, yet I knew

He will wipe every tear from their eyes. There won't be any more death. There won't be any grief, crying, or pain, because the first things have disappeared.

Revelation 21:4 GW

that if I had, that too would have been more glorious than anything I had eaten or drunk on earth. The best way I can explain it is to say that I felt as if I were in another dimension. Never, even in my happiest moments, had I ever felt so fully alive. I stood speechless in front of the crowd of loved ones, still trying to take in everything. Over and over I heard how overjoyed they were to see me and how excited they were to have me among them. I'm not sure if they actually said the words or not, but I knew they had been waiting and expecting me, yet I also knew that in heaven there is no sense of time passing.

I gazed at all the faces again as I realized that they all had contributed to my becoming a Christian or had encouraged me in my growth as a believer. Each one had affected me positively. Each had spiritually impacted me in some way and helped make me a better disciple. I knew—again one of those things I knew without being aware of how I had absorbed that information—that because of their influence I was able to be present with them in heaven.

We didn't talk about what they had done for me. Our conversations centered on the joy of my being there and how happy they were to see me.

Still overwhelmed, I didn't know how to respond to their welcoming words. "I'm happy to be with you," I said, and even those words couldn't express the utter joy of being surrounded and embraced by all those people I loved.

I wasn't conscious of anything I'd left behind and felt no regrets about leaving family or possessions. It was as if God had removed anything negative or worrisome from my consciousness, and I could only rejoice at being together with these wonderful people.

They looked exactly as I once knew them—although they were more radiant and joyful than they'd ever been on earth.

As I stared at her beaming face, I sensed that age has no meaning in heaven.

My great-grandmother, Hattie Mann, was Native American. As a child I saw her only after she had developed osteoporosis. Her head and shoulders were bent forward, giving her a humped

46

appearance. I especially remember her extremely wrinkled face. The other thing that stands out in my memory is that she had false teeth—which she didn't wear often. Yet when she smiled at me in heaven, her teeth sparkled. I knew they were her own, and when she smiled, it was the most beautiful smile I had ever seen.

Then I noticed something else—she wasn't slumped over. She stood strong and upright, and the wrinkles had been erased from her face. I have no idea what age she was, and I didn't even think about that. As I stared at her beaming face, I sensed that age has no meaning in heaven.

Age expresses time passing, and there is no time there. All of the people I encountered were the same age they had been the last time I had seen them—except that all the ravages of living on earth had vanished. Even though some of their features may not have been considered attractive on earth, in heaven every feature was perfect, beautiful, and wonderful to gaze at.

Even now, years later, I can sometimes close my eyes and see those perfect countenances and smiles that surprised me with the most human warmth and friendliness I've ever witnessed. Just being with them was a holy moment and remains a treasured hope.

When I first stood in heaven, they were still in front of me and came rushing toward me. They embraced me, and no matter which direction I looked, I saw someone I had loved and who had loved me. They surrounded me, moving around so that everyone had a chance to welcome me to heaven.

I felt loved—more loved than ever before in my life. They didn't say they loved me. I don't remember what words they spoke. When they gazed at me, I *knew* what the Bible means by perfect love. It emanated from every person who surrounded me.

Even now, years later, I can sometimes close my eyes and see those perfect countenances and smiles.

I stared at them, and as I did I felt as if I absorbed their love for me. At some point, I looked around and the sight overwhelmed me. Everything was brilliantly intense. Coming out from the gate—a short distance ahead—was a brilliance that was brighter than the light that surrounded us, utterly luminous. As soon as I stopped gazing at the people's faces, I realized that everything around me glowed with a dazzling intensity. In trying to describe the scene, words are totally inadequate, because human words can't express the feelings of awe and wonder at what I beheld.

Everything I saw glowed with intense brightness. The best I can describe it is that we began to move toward that light. No one said it was time to do so, and yet we all started forward at the same time. As I stared ahead, everything seemed to grow taller— like a gentle hill that kept going upward and never stopped. I had expected to see some darkness behind the gate, but as far ahead as I could see, there was absolutely nothing but intense, radiant light.

By contrast, the powerful light I had encountered when I met my friends and loved ones paled into darkness as the radiance and iridescence in front of me increased. It was as if each step I took intensified the glowing luminosity. I didn't know how it could get more dazzling, but it did. It would be like cracking open the door of a dark room and walking into the brightness of a noonday sun. As the door swings open, the full rays of the sun burst forth, and we're momentarily blinded.

I wasn't blinded, but I was amazed that the luster and intensity continually increased. Strange as it seems, as brilliant as everything was, each time I stepped forward, the splendor increased. The farther I walked, the brighter the light. The light engulfed me, and I had the sense that I was being ushered into the presence of God. Although our earthly eyes must gradually adjust to light or darkness, my heavenly eyes saw with absolute ease. In heaven, each of our senses is immeasurably heightened to take it all in. And what a sensory celebration!

A holy awe came over me as I stepped forward. I had no idea what lay ahead, but I sensed that with each step I took, it would grow more wondrous.

Then I heard the music.

3

Heavenly Music

Then I looked again, and I heard the
singing of thousands and millions
of angels around the throne and the
living beings and the elders.

Revelation 5:11

As a young boy I spent a lot of time out in the country and woods. When walking through waist-high dried grass, I often surprised a covey of birds and flushed them out of their nests on the ground. A whooshing sound accompanied their wings as they flew away.

My most vivid memory of heaven is what I heard. I can only describe it as a holy swoosh of wings.

But I'd have to magnify that thousands of times to explain the effect of the sound in heaven.

It was the most beautiful and pleasant sound I've ever heard, and it didn't stop. It was like a song that goes on forever. I felt awestruck, wanting only to listen. I didn't just hear music. It seemed as if I were part of the music—and it played in and through my body. I stood still, and yet I felt embraced by the sounds.

> *I didn't just hear music. It seemed as if I were part of the music. . . .*

As aware as I became of the joyous sounds and melodies that filled the air, I wasn't distracted. I felt as if the heavenly concert permeated every part of my being, and at the same time I focused on everything else around me.

I never saw anything that produced the sound. I had the sense that whatever made the heavenly music was just above me, but I didn't look up. I'm not sure why. Perhaps it was because I was so enamored with the people around me, or maybe it was because my senses were so engaged that I feasted on everything at the same time. I asked no questions and never wondered about anything. Everything was perfect. I sensed that I knew everything and had no questions to ask.

A myriad of sounds so filled my mind and heart that it's difficult to explain them. The most amazing one, however, was the angels' wings. I didn't see them, but the sound was a beautiful, holy melody with a cadence that seemed never to stop. The swishing resounded as if it was a form of

never-ending praise. As I listened I simply
knew what it was.

A second sound remains, even today,
the single most vivid memory I have of my
entire heavenly experience. I call it music,
but it differed from anything I had ever
heard or ever expect to hear on the earth.
The melodies of praise filled the atmosphere.
The nonstop intensity and endless variety
overwhelmed me.

The praise was unending, but the
most remarkable thing to me was that
hundreds of songs were being sung at the
same time—all of them worshiping God.
As I approached the large, magnificent
gate, I heard them from every direction
and realized that each voice praised God.
I write *voice,* but it was more than that.

When he falls, he will

not be thrown down

headfirst

because the LORD holds

on to his hand.

Psalm 37:24 GW

Some sounded instrumental, but I wasn't sure—and I wasn't concerned. Praise was everywhere, and all of it was musical, yet comprised of melodies and tones I'd never experienced before.

Hymns of praise, modern-sounding choruses, and ancient chants filled my ears.

"Hallelujah!" "Praise!" "Glory to God!" "Praise to the King!" Such words rang out in the midst of all the music. I don't know if angels were singing them or if they came from humans. I felt so awestruck and caught up in the heavenly mood that I didn't look around. My heart filled with the deepest joy I've ever experienced. I wasn't a participant in the worship, yet I felt as if my heart rang out with the same kind of joy and exuberance.

If we played three CDs of praise at the same time, we'd have a cacophony of noise that would drive us crazy. This was totally different. Every sound blended, and each voice or instrument enhanced the others.

As strange as it may seem, I could clearly distinguish each song. It sounded as if each hymn of praise was meant for me to hear as I moved inside the gates.

Many of the old hymns and choruses I had sung at various times in my life were part of the music—along with hundreds of songs I had never heard before. Hymns of praise, modern-sounding choruses, and ancient chants filled my ears and brought not only a deep peace but the greatest feeling of joy I've ever experienced.

As I stood before the gate, I didn't think of it, but later I realized that I didn't hear such songs as "The Old Rugged Cross" or "The Nail-Scarred Hand." None of the hymns that filled the air were about Jesus's sacrifice or death. I heard no sad songs and instinctively knew that there are no sad songs in heaven. Why would there be? All were praises about Christ's reign as King of Kings and our joyful worship for all he has done for us and how wonderful he is.

The celestial tunes surpassed any I had ever heard. I couldn't calculate the number of songs—perhaps thousands—offered up simultaneously, and yet there was no chaos, because I had the capacity to hear each one and discern the lyrics and melody.

I marveled at the glorious music. Though not possessed of a great singing voice in life, I knew that if I sang, my voice would be in perfect pitch and would sound as melodious and harmonious as the thousands of other voices and instruments that filled my ears.

Even now, back on earth, sometimes I still hear faint echoes of that music. When I'm especially tired and lie in bed with my eyes closed, occasionally I drift off to sleep with the sounds of heaven filling my heart and mind. No matter how difficult a day I've had, peace immediately fills every part of my being. I still have flashbacks, although they're different from what we normally refer to as flashbacks. Mine are more flashbacks of the sounds than the sights.

As I've pondered the meaning of the memory of the music, it seems curious. I would have expected the most memorable experience to be something I had seen or the physical embrace of a loved one. Yet above everything else, I cherish those sounds, and at times I think, *I can't wait to hear them again—in person*. It's what I look forward to. I want to see everybody, but I know I'll be with them forever. I want to experience everything heaven offers, but most of all, I want to hear those never-ending songs again.

> *Yet above everything else, I cherish those sounds, and at times I think,* I can't wait to hear them again—in person.

Obviously, I can't really know how God feels, but I find joy and comfort in thinking that he must be pleased and blessed by the continuous sounds of praise.

In those minutes—and they held no sense of time for me—others touched me, and their warm embraces were absolutely real. I saw colors I would never have believed existed. I've never, ever felt more alive than I did then.

I was home; I was where I belonged. I wanted to be there more than I had ever wanted to be anywhere on earth. Time had slipped away, and I was simply present in heaven. All worries, anxieties, and concerns vanished. I had no needs, and I felt perfect.

I get frustrated describing what heaven was like, because I can't begin to put into words what it looked like, sounded like, and felt like. It was perfect, and I knew I had no needs and never would again. I didn't even think of earth or those left behind.

I did not see God. Although I knew God was there, I never saw any kind of image or luminous glow to indicate his divine presence. I've heard people talk about going inside and coming back out the gate. That didn't happen to me.

I saw only a bright iridescence. I peered through the gate, yearning to see what lay beyond. It wasn't an anxious yearning, but a peaceful openness to experience all the grace and joy of heaven.

The only way I've made sense out of that part of the experience is to think that if I had actually seen God, I would never have wanted to return. My feeling has been that once we're actually in God's presence, we will never return to earth again, because it will be empty and meaningless by comparison.

> *"To be absent from the body is to be present with the Lord to those who love him and know him." I believed those words before. I believe them even more now.*

For me, just to reach the gates was amazing. It was a foretaste of joy divine. My

Don't pray for tasks
equal to your pow-
ers; pray for power
equal to your tasks.

Phillips Brooks

words are too feeble to describe what took place.

As a pastor, I've stood at the foot of many caskets and done many funerals and said, "To be absent from the body is to be present with the Lord to those who love him and know him."

I believed those words before. I believe them even more now.

After a time (I'm resorting to human terms again), we started moving together right up to the gate. No one said it, but I simply knew God had sent all those people to escort me inside the portals of heaven.

Looming just over the heads of my reception committee stood an awesome gate interrupting a wall that faded out of sight in both directions. It struck me that the actual entrance was small in comparison to the massive gate itself. I stared, but I couldn't see the ends of the walls in either direction. As I gazed upward, I couldn't see the top either.

One thing did surprise me: On earth, whenever I thought of heaven, I anticipated that one day I'd see a gate made of pearls, because the Bible refers to the gates of pearl. The gate wasn't made of pearls, but was pearlescent—perhaps *iridescent* may be more descriptive. To me, it looked as if someone had spread pearl icing on a cake. The gate glowed and shimmered.

I paused and stared at the glorious hues and shimmering shades. The luminescence dazzled me, and I would have been content to stay at that spot. Yet I stepped forward as if being escorted into God's presence.

I paused just outside the gate, and I could see inside. It was like a city with paved streets. To my amazement, they had been constructed of literal gold. If you imagine a street paved with gold bricks, that's as close as I can come to describing what lay inside the gate.

The closer we got, the more intense, alive, and vivid everything became.

Everything I saw was bright—the brightest colors my eyes had ever beheld— so powerful that no earthly human could take in this brilliance.

In the midst of that powerful scene, I continued to step closer to the gate and assumed that I would go inside. My friends and relatives were all in front of me, calling, urging, and inviting me to follow.

Then the scene changed. I can explain it only by saying that instead of their being in front of me, they were beside me. I felt that they wanted to walk beside me as I passed through the iridescent gate.

Sometimes people have asked me, "How did you move? Did you walk? Did you float?" I don't know. I just moved along with that welcoming crowd. As we came closer to the gate, the music increased and became even more vivid. It would be like walking up to a glorious event after hearing the faint sounds and seeing everything from a distance. The closer we got, the more intense, alive, and vivid everything became.

Just as I reached the gate, my senses were
even more heightened, and I felt deliriously
happy.

I paused—I'm not sure why—just
outside the gate. I was thrilled at the
prospect and wanted to go inside. I knew
everything would be even more thrilling
than what I had experienced so far. At
that very moment I was about to realize
the yearning of every human heart. I was
in heaven and ready to go in through the
pearlescent gate.

During that momentary pause,
something else changed. Instead of just
hearing the music and the thousands of
voices praising God, I had become part of
the choir. I was one with them, and they
had absorbed me into their midst. I had

arrived at a place I had wanted to visit for a long time; I lingered to gaze before I continued forward.

Then, just as suddenly as I had arrived at the gates of heaven, I left them.

4

From Heaven to Earth

Even when I walk
    through the dark valley of death,
I will not be afraid,
    for you are close beside me.
Your rod and your staff
    protect and comfort me.

Psalm 23:4

The EMTs pronounced me dead as soon as they arrived at the scene. They stated that I died instantly. According to the report, the collision occurred at 11:45 A.M. The EMTs became so busy working with the others involved that it was about 1:15 P.M. before they were ready to move me. They checked for a pulse once again.

I was still dead.

The state law said they had to pronounce me dead officially before they could remove my body from the scene of the accident. Unless they declared me dead, an ambulance would have to transport my body to a hospital. That county didn't have a coroner, but I learned later that a justice of the peace could declare me dead, and then they could remove my body.

Because I was dead, there seemed to be no need for speed. Their concern focused on clearing the bridge for traffic to flow again.

Ambulances had come from the prison, the county, and Huntsville. Except for one, all of them left without taking back any patients. The last one was preparing to leave. From information I've pieced together, someone had arranged for an unmarked vehicle to take my body to a mortuary.

They had called for the Jaws of Life[1] to get me out of the smashed car. Because I was dead, there seemed to be no need for speed. Their concern focused on clearing the bridge for traffic to flow again.

When the truck came in at an angle and went right over the top of me, the truck smashed the car's ceiling, and the dashboard came down across my legs, crushing my right leg. My left leg was shattered in two places between the car seat and the dashboard. My left arm went over the top of my head, was dislocated, and swung backward over the seat. It was still attached—barely.

That left arm had been lying on the driver's side door, because I had been driving with my right hand. As I would learn later, the major bones were now missing, so my lower left arm was just a piece of flesh that held the hand to the rest of the arm. It was the same with the left leg. There was some tissue just above my knee that still fed blood to the calf and foot below. Four and a half inches of femur were missing and never found. The doctors have no medical explanation why I didn't lose all the blood in my body.

Glass and blood had sprayed everywhere. I had all kinds of small holes in my face from embedded glass. The steering wheel had pounded into my chest. Blood seeped out of my eyes, ears, and nose.

Just from seeing the results of the crash, the EMTs knew I had to have sustained massive head injuries and that my insides

We understand what love is when we realize that Christ gave his life for us. That means we must give our lives for other believers. Now, suppose a person has enough to live on and notices another believer in need. How can God's love be in that person if he doesn't bother to help the other believer?

1 John 3:16–17 GW

were completely rearranged. When he first felt no pulse, one of the EMTs covered me with a waterproof tarp that also blocked off the top of the car. They made no attempt to move me or try to get me out immediately—they couldn't have anyway, because it would have been impossible for them to drag or lift me out of the vehicle without the Jaws of Life.

One thing that sped help to the scene was that the two prison guards in the pickup truck immediately called for emergency assistance from the prison. Otherwise, we would have been too far away for any emergency vehicle to get to us quickly.

They examined the drivers of the other two cars; both of them were uninjured and

refused medical attention. The prisoner
who drove the truck sustained no injuries.
As soon as the EMTs determined he was all
right, they transported
him back to the prison.
Police halted all traffic on
the bridge and waited for
the ambulance to arrive.
While they waited,
traffic backed up for
miles in both directions,
especially the direction
I had come from. It was
only a narrow two-lane
bridge, not wide enough
for a car to turn around.

*One thing that sped
help to the scene was
that the two prison
guards in the pickup
truck immediately
called for emergency
assistance from
the prison.*

Even if the waiting traffic could have turned
around, they would have had to drive an

We, however, are citizens of heaven. We look forward to the Lord Jesus Christ coming from heaven as our Savior. Through his power to bring everything under his authority, he will change our humble bodies and make them like his glorified body.

Philippians 3:20–21 GW

extra forty or fifty miles around the lake
to reach another road leading to their
destination.

From the backed-up traffic, Dick and
Anita Onarecker walked at least half a
mile to the scene of the accident. Dick
and Anita had started a church in Klein,
which is north of Houston. Both had
spoken at the conference I'd just attended.
I'm not positive we actually met at Trinity
Pines, although we may have. For years
I had heard of Dick Onarecker, but that
conference was the first time I had ever seen
him.

On Wednesday morning, the Onareckers
left Trinity Pines a few minutes before I
did. By Houston standards, that January
morning was extremely cold. As they sped

along, Anita said, "I'm really chilled. Could we stop for coffee? I think that would warm me up."

Dick spotted a bait shop right on Lake Livingston, so they pulled over. Apparently, while they were buying coffee, I drove past them.

When they saw a police officer, Dick said, "I'm a minister. Is there anybody here I can help? Is there anyone I can pray for?"

Many times afterward, Dick would bury his face in his hands and say, "You know that could easily have been us. It should have been us, but because we stopped and you drove past us, you got hit."

Before the Onareckers reached the bridge, the accident had occurred and traffic had started to back up. People got out of their cars and milled around, asking questions and sharing their limited information.

After Dick and Anita got out of their car, they asked fellow drivers, "What's going on up there?"

The word had passed down that there had been a serious auto accident. "A truck crashed into a car" was about all anyone knew.

Dick and Anita stood around a few minutes, but nothing happened, and more cars lined up behind them. Sometime between 12:30 and 12:45, they decided to walk to the accident site. When they saw a police officer, Dick said, "I'm a minister.

Is there anybody here I can help? Is there anyone I can pray for?"

The police officer shook his head. "The people in those two cars," he said and pointed, "are shaken up a little bit but they're fine. Talk to them if you'd like."

"What about the other vehicle? The one with the tarp over it?"

"The man in the red car is deceased."

While Dick talked to the officer, Anita went over to the other vehicles. She gave her barely touched coffee to the old man.

Dick would later tell it this way: "God spoke to me and said, 'You need to pray for the man in the red car.'" Dick was an outstanding Baptist preacher. Praying for a dead man certainly ran counter to his theology. *I can't do that,* he thought. *How can I go over there and pray? The man is dead.*

The rain had become a light drizzle, but Dick was oblivious to his surroundings. Dick stared at the officer, knowing that what he would say wouldn't make sense. Yet God spoke to him so clearly that he had no doubt about what he was to do. God had told him to pray for a dead man. As bizarre as that seemed to him, Dick also had no doubt that the Holy Spirit was prompting him to act.

"I'd like to pray for the man in the red car," Dick finally said to the officer.

"Like I said, he's dead."

"I know this sounds strange, but I want to pray for him anyway."

The officer stared at him a long time before he finally said, "Well, you know, if that's what you want to do, go ahead, but I've got to tell you it's an awful sight. He's dead, and it's really a mess under the tarp. Blood and glass are everywhere, and the body's all mangled."

Dick, then in his forties, said, "I was a medic in Vietnam, so the idea of blood doesn't bother me."

"I have to warn you—" The man stopped, shrugged, and said, "Do what you want, but I'll

From the pictures of that smashed-down car, it's almost impossible to believe, but somehow Dick actually crawled into the trunk of my Ford ... [and] began praying for me.

tell you that you haven't seen anybody this bad."

"Thanks," Dick said, and walked to the tarp-covered car.

From the pictures of that smashed-down car, it's almost impossible to believe, but somehow Dick actually crawled into the trunk of my Ford. It had been a hatchback, but that part of the car had been severed. I was still covered by the tarp, which he didn't remove, so it was extremely dark inside the car. Dick crept in behind me, leaned over the backseat, and put his hand on my right shoulder.

He began praying for me. As he said later, "I felt compelled to pray. I didn't know who the man was or whether he was a believer. I knew only that God told me I had to pray for him."

As Dick prayed, he became quite emotional and broke down and cried several times. Then he sang. Dick had an excellent voice and often sang publicly. He paused several times to sing a hymn and then went back to prayer.

Not only did Dick believe God had called him to pray for me but he prayed quite specifically that I would be delivered from unseen injuries, meaning brain and internal injuries.

This sounds strange, because Dick knew I was dead. Not only had the police officer told him but he also had checked for a pulse. He had no idea why he prayed as he did, except God told him to. He didn't pray for the injuries he could see, only for the healing of internal damage. He said

There will no longer be any curse. The throne of God and the lamb will be in the city. His servants will worship him and see his face. His name will be on their foreheads. There will be no more night, and they will not need any light from lamps or the sun because the Lord God will shine on them. They will rule as kings forever and ever.

Revelation 22:3–5 GW

he prayed the most passionate, fervent, emotional prayer of his life. As I would later learn, Dick was a highly emotional man anyway.

Then he began to sing again. "O what peace we often forfeit, O what needless pain we bear, all because we do not carry everything to God in prayer!"[2] The only thing I personally know for certain about the entire event is that as he sang the blessed old hymn "What a Friend We Have in Jesus," I began to sing with him.

In that first moment of consciousness, I was aware of two things. First, I was singing—a different kind of singing than the tones of heaven—I heard my own voice and then became aware of someone else singing.

The second thing I was aware of was that someone clutched my hand. It was a strong, powerful touch and the first physical sensation I experienced with my return to earthly life.

More than a year would lapse before I understood the significance of that hand clasping mine.

I was privileged to share the story of my recovery in Dick's church, Klein First Baptist, a little more than a year after the accident. His wife, Anita, was there, and so was my own family. Because I still wore leg braces, two people had to help me walk up on the platform.

I told everyone about the accident and about Dick's part in bringing me back.

If any of you needs wisdom to know what you should do, you should ask God, and he will give it to you. God is generous to everyone and doesn't find fault with them. When you ask for something, don't have any doubts. A person who has doubts is like a wave that is blown by the wind and tossed by the sea. A person who has doubts shouldn't expect to receive anything from the Lord. A person who has doubts is thinking about two different things at the same time and can't make up his mind about anything.

James 1:5–8 GW

"I believe I'm alive today because Dick prayed me back to earth," I said. "In my first moments of consciousness, two things stand out. First, I was singing 'What a Friend We Have in Jesus.' The second was that Dick's hand gripped mine and held it tight."

After the morning worship, many of us went out to lunch together at a Chinese restaurant. Anita sat across from me. I remember sipping my wonton soup and having a delightful time with the church members.

When there was a lull in the conversation, Anita leaned across the table and said in a low voice, "I appreciated everything you said this morning."

"Thank you—"

"There's just one thing—one thing I need to correct about what you said in your message."

"Really?" Her words shocked me. "I tried to be as accurate as possible in everything I said. I certainly didn't intend to exaggerate anything. What did I say that was incorrect?"

"You were talking about Dick getting into the car with you. Then you said he prayed for you while he was holding your hand."

"Yes, I remember that part very distinctly. I have a number of memory gaps, and most of the things I don't remember." That morning I had readily admitted that some of the information I gave came secondhand. "The one thing that's totally clear was Dick being in the car and praying with me."

"That's true. He did get in the car and pray with you." She leaned closer. "But, Don, he never held your hand."

"I distinctly remember holding his hand."

"That didn't happen. It was physically impossible."

"But I remember that so clearly. It's one of the most vivid—"

"Think about it. Dick leaned over from the rear of the trunk over the backseat and put his hand on your shoulder and touched you. You were facing forward, and your left arm was barely hanging together."

"Yes, that's true."

"Dick said you were slumped over on the seat toward the passenger side."

I closed my eyes, visualizing what she had just said. I nodded.

"Your hand was on the floor of the passenger side of the car. Although the tarp covered the car, there was enough light for him to see your hand down there. There was no way Dick could have reached your right hand."

"But . . . but . . ." I sputtered.

"Someone was holding your hand. But it wasn't Dick."

"If it wasn't Dick's hand, whose was it?"

She smiled and said, "I think you know."

I put down my spoon and stared at her for several seconds. I had no doubt whatsoever that someone had held my hand. Then I understood. "Yes, I think I know too."

5

The *Why* Questions

Now we see things imperfectly as
in a poor mirror, but then we will
see everything with perfect clarity.
All that I know now is partial and
incomplete, but then I will know
everything completely, just as God
knows me now.

1 Corinthians 13:12

Many times I've watched people on TV who say they've had near-death experiences (NDE). I confess to being fascinated, but I also admit to being skeptical. In fact, I'm highly skeptical. Before and after those people spoke, I thought, *They've probably had some kind of brain lapse. Or maybe there was already something in their memory bank and they just re-experienced it.* I didn't doubt their sincerity; they wanted to believe what they talked about.

I've watched many talk shows and read about victims who had died and been heroically resuscitated. Descriptions of their ordeals often seemed too rehearsed and disturbingly similar, as if one person copied the story of the last. One person who claimed to have been dead for more than twenty-four hours wrote a book and said he had talked to Adam and Eve. Some of the things the first earthly couple purportedly told him don't measure up with the Bible.

> *Despite my skepticism—even today—of many of their testimonies, I have never questioned my own death.*

Despite my skepticism—even today—of many of their testimonies, I have never questioned my own death. In fact, it was so powerful, so life changing, that I couldn't talk about it to anyone until my closest friend, David Gentiles, pried out the information almost two years after the accident.

I have looked at the research on NDE and thought about it often during the years.

In December 2001, *Lancet*, the journal of the British Medical Society, reported research on NDE. Most scientific and medical experts had previously dismissed these dramatic occurrences as wishful thinking or the misguided musings of oxygen-starved brains.

The study, conducted in the Netherlands, is one of the first scientific studies on NDE. Instead of interviewing those who reported they had once had an NDE, they

Turn to God and change

the way you think and

act, because the king-

dom of heaven is near.

Matthew 3:2 GW

followed hundreds of patients who had been resuscitated after suffering clinical death—that is, after their hearts stopped. They hoped that approach would provide more accurate accounts by documenting the experiences as they happened, rather than basing them on recollections long after the event of resuscitation.

Their results: About 18 percent of the patients in the study spoke of recollection of the time in which they had been clinically dead. Between 8 and 12 percent reported the commonly accepted NDE experiences, such as seeing bright lights, going through a tunnel, or even crossing over into heaven and speaking with dead relatives and friends. The researchers concluded that afterlife experiences or

NDE are merely "something we would all desperately like to believe is true."[1]

Conversely, other scholars made conclusions based on their study of 344 people (ages twenty-six to ninety-two) who had been resuscitated. Most of them were interviewed within five days of the experience. The researchers contacted those same people two years later and then eight years after the event.

> *Those who had such experiences reported marked changes in their personalities. . . . They became more compassionate, giving, and loving.*

Researchers discovered that the experiences didn't correlate with any of the measured psychological, physiological, or medical parameters—that is, the experiences were unrelated to processes in the dying brain. Most patients had excellent recall of the events, which, the researchers said, undermined the idea that the memories were false.

The most important thing to me is that those who had such experiences reported marked changes in their personalities. They lost their fear of death. They became more compassionate, giving, and loving.

The study really proved nothing about the reality of NDE. As had been the case before the studies, one group believed NDE were merely the psychological states of those dying; the other group maintained that hard evidence supported the validity of near-death occurrences, suggesting that scientists rethink theories that dismiss out-of-body experiences.

I have no intention of trying to solve this debate. I can only relate what happened to me. No matter what researchers may or may not try to tell me, I *know* I went to heaven.

I've devoted an immense amount of time to considering *why* it happened rather than *what* happened. I have reached only one solid conclusion: Before being killed in a car accident, I remained skeptical of near-death experiences. I simply didn't see how a person could die, go to heaven, and return to tell about it. I never doubted dying, the reality of heaven, or life after death. I doubted descriptions of near-death stories. These stories all seemed too rehearsed and sounded alike. Then I died, went to heaven,

Christianity demands
a level of caring that
transcends human
inclination.

Erwin Lutzer

and returned. I can only tell what happened to me. Not for an instant have I ever thought it was merely a vision, some case of mental wires crossing, or the result of stories I'd heard. I *know* heaven is real. I have been there and come back.

"Now when I hear you talk about heaven's beauty, I understand a little better why you'd willingly be separated from my daughter and grandkids for a while."

It comes down to this: Until some mere mortal is dead for a lengthy period and subsequently returns to life with irrefutable evidence of an afterlife, near-death experiences will continue to be a matter of faith, or at the very least, conjecture. But then, as

112

one of my friends would say, "What else is new?"

⎯⎯∞⎯⎯

One time I shared my experiences with a large congregation that included my wife's parents, Eldon and Ethel Pentecost. They've been consistently supportive and made great sacrifices during my accident and lengthy recovery.

After the service, we went to their home. At one point, Eldon and I were alone, and he told me, "I was angry the first time you shared your story of your trip to heaven."

I had no idea he felt that way.

"You finished by saying you never wanted to come back to earth."

I just nodded in affirmation, not knowing where this was going.

It takes a true believer
to be compassionate.
No greater burden can
be borne by an indi-
vidual than to know
that no one cares or
understands.

Arthur Stainback

"I didn't understand it then, but I've changed. Now when I hear you talk about heaven's beauty, I understand a little better why you'd willingly be separated from my daughter and grandkids for a while. You know—you really do know, don't you— that they'll join you someday?"

"Without a doubt," I said.

Eldon's revelation caught me off guard. He was right, of course. I had the distinct privilege of baptizing my own children and seeing my wife baptized as well. I knew that their professions of faith were authentic. By faith, I knew that they would be residents of heaven someday. Being separated from them had never crossed my mind while I was in heaven. People in heaven simply don't have an awareness of who is *not* there. They do know who is coming.

Even today, I can say honestly that I wish I could have stayed in heaven, but my ultimate time had not yet come. After leaving heaven, if I had known that I would face two weeks in ICU, a year in a hospital bed, and thirty-four operations, I surely would have been even more disheartened from the outset. However, this was not my choice, and I returned to the sounds of one voice praying, boots crunching glass underfoot, and the Jaws of Life ripping through my shattered auto.

One question keeps troubling me: *Why?* It takes many forms.

Why did I die in that car wreck?

Why did I have the unique privilege of going to heaven?

Why did I glimpse heaven, only to be sent back?

Why did I nearly die in the hospital?

Why has God let me live in constant pain since January 18, 1989?

> *I do know God is with me in the darkest moments of life.*

The short answer: I don't know. And yet that single word, *why*, remains the consummate human query. By nature, we're curious. We want to know.

All these years later, it's still not easy for me to relate what happened. Several times I tried to write this myself but couldn't. That's why I asked my friend Cec Murphey to help me with this book—if it were up to me, this book would never have been written. The emotional trauma of reliving all the events is too difficult. Only with someone else actually writing it has it finally been possible to go through this ordeal.

I still don't know why such things happen.

I do know God is with me in the darkest moments of life.

Besides asking why, there are other questions. I think they're even more important for me to ponder.

Did God want me to know how real pain could feel so that I could understand the pain of others?

Did God want me to know how real heaven is?

The man who says
his prayers at night
is a captain posting
his sentinels. He
can sleep.

Baudelaire

What did God want me to learn from all my experiences, my death, and the long period of recovery?

How can my experiences be of the most benefit to others?

After all these years, I don't have the answers to most of those questions, either. I have learned a few things and realize that God still has reasons for keeping me alive on earth. I may never know his reasons, and God has no obligation to explain them to me.

Even though I don't have full answers to many of my questions, I do have peace. I know I am where God wants me to be. I know I'm doing the work God has given me.

I find comfort in a story recorded in John's Gospel. A man born blind meets Jesus and is healed. After that, he runs around praising God, but his healing is an embarrassment to the religious leaders who have been trying to turn the people against Jesus. They interrogate the formerly blind man, trying to force him to admit that Jesus is a sinner (that is, a fraud).

The man wisely says, "Whether he is a sinner or not, I don't know. One thing I do know. I was blind but now I see!" (John 9:25 NIV). In the same way, some may not believe my account; they may think it was some kind of wish fulfillment during a point of severe trauma. I don't have to defend my experience.

I know what happened to me. For those of us whose faith is in the reality of heaven, no amount of evidence is necessary. *I know what I experienced.*

I believe God gave me a hint of what eternity in heaven will be like.

I also believe that part of the reason I am still alive, as I've already pointed out, is that people prayed. Dick Onarecker prayed me back to life—to live without brain damage. David Gentiles and others prayed so that God wouldn't take me back to heaven just yet.

I am here, I am alive, and it's because God's purposes have not yet been fulfilled in my life. When God is finished with me, I'll return to the place I yearn to be. I have made my final reservations for heaven, and I'm going back someday—permanently.

Prayerfully, I'll see you there too.

A Final Word

The elderly woman waited at the back of the book signing line until everyone else had gone. Timidly she approached and held out her book to me to sign. As I started to write, she bent down and spoke barely above a whisper. "I need to ask you something."

I looked up and gazed into pale blue eyes, which were flooded with tears. I smiled, nodded, and waited for her to speak.

"Is my Gene all right? Is he happy? Does he miss me?" She told me that Gene died a few months after their sixtieth wedding anniversary. They were both Christians and had been active in their church for all of those years.

"I can assure you that Gene is totally happy and that he doesn't miss you," I said. "If he missed you, how could he be happy? But I can also tell you that when you die, Gene will stand among the joyful crowd waiting at heaven's gate to meet you."

We must have talked another five or six minutes. She smiled, thanked me for signing her book, and kissed my cheek. "I miss him every day, but to know that he's happy gives me comfort."

She was just one person who came with questions. There have been many, many others. Although the response to my story has been personally humbling and overwhelming, the worldwide impact has been incredible and amazingly positive. Many times, crowds have jammed large auditoriums and tents. At other times, a few dozen sat and listened intently while I shared my experience. Yet each time, the private moments afterward meant the most to me. Often, it's meeting someone new with whom I will spend eternity—someone like Gene's widow.

Many anguished souls will share tearful personal confessions and seek assurance of forgiveness. It's as if they need to know they're not too bad for God to forgive. And they need to know that no one is too bad or sinful for God to forgive. Others struggle with personal problems or yearn for a better life. They're the ones with whom I like to talk. They hurt and they want relief. They want the kind of peace that comes only through Jesus Christ.

I spent less than two hours in heaven, but those ninety minutes were enough to make me aware of the glory that lies ahead for all believers in Jesus Christ. God sent me back to earth, and my heavenly experience has enabled me to bring comfort to many.

I also want to say that those encounters, along with thousands of emails, letters, and phone calls, have humbled me and enriched my life beyond measure.

I hope this book has provided comfort and assurance to you if you're a Christian. By that I mean, that if you believe that Jesus Christ died to take away your sins and you commit your life to following him on this earth, I can speak with total confidence of the blessedness and the perfection of a life that never ends.

For those who wonder about loved ones who have died, I can assure you that all believers are serenely happy and filled with what the apostle Peter calls "joy unspeakable and full of glory,"[1] as they wait for their loved ones to gather with them.

I wrote about my experience, and many have already found help as they look toward the time when they too must pass from this earthly existence to the life eternal.

That book wasn't written only to assure people of their future—although that's true. A second reason I wrote *90 Minutes in Heaven* was to encourage and comfort those who grieve. When we lose those whom we love, we miss them, and there remains a hole in our lives. Nothing can bring them back, but I can report about the perfection and the immeasurable happiness of those who are already inside the gates of heaven.

I am blessed to be able to bring universal answers to the issue of life after death— answers to the questions many wonder about. We want our lives to be meaningful after a tragedy or loss; we want to know what lies ahead; we want the assurance of eternal life. Because I've been there and come back, I can offer solid hope as I relay the realities of heaven.

As part of my recovery from the accident, I was bedridden, underwent more than thirty surgeries, faced a questionable future, and seemed to have more questions than answers, especially about the purpose of my life. As a result of the amazing response to *90 Minutes in Heaven*, at least some of those questions have been answered. Each time I hold the hand of despondent individuals and pray with them; each time I give an altar call after preaching from Sweden to Shreveport and throngs come forward; each time people wipe away their tears because they realize that the separation from a loved one is only temporary—I know I will spend the remainder of my earthly pilgrimage bringing hope and comfort.

I hope I'll cross paths with each of you this side of glory. If that is not to be, I'll wait to see you at the gate!

Stories of Encouragement

Fred's Legacy

In 2007, Fred Winters, pastor of First Baptist Church in Maryville, Illinois, invited me to speak. I was unable to make my schedule fit with his, so we set it up for the far-off date of Sunday evening, April 26, 2009.

I never got to meet Fred.

About 8:15 on Sunday morning, March 8, 2009—less than six weeks before I was scheduled to speak—a man shot Fred Winters inside the church shortly after the worship service began. They rushed him to the hospital but he had died instantly.

When I learned about Fred's death, I was preaching in Hawaii. I called the Maryville church immediately. Because they were flooded with incoming calls, no one on the staff was able to talk with me; however, about an hour later, Cindy Carnes, the church's business administrator, called back. I expressed my profound condolences. "I will be all right if you want to postpone my coming—"

"No! We need you now more than ever and Fred wanted you to come," she said.

"I'll be there," I said. "Anything I can do for you in the meantime?"

"Pray for us; we've never buried a pastor before."

Something about the way she spoke and the words she spoke burned in my heart. Inside my head, I can still hear the pain and confusion in her voice.

When I arrived at the church on the evening of April 26, their parking lots were completely filled. I saw no vacant seats in the church sanctuary, which seated three thousand. The choir started the service; they wore red shirts and black pants.

"Fred Winters has to be smiling down on the congregation to witness what he sees here," I said during my message. I reminded them that Fred was in heaven because he had chosen to go there years earlier. "Heaven is a prepared place for prepared people." I talked to them about being ready for heaven.

Mark Jones, a minister at the church, said later to a reporter, "The twofold approach of having Don Piper talking about heaven and what Pastor Fred was experiencing brought incredible healing to our congregation."

Mark said something else that I liked: "Pastor Fred would have been thrilled about having all the people at that meeting, but I think he would have asked, 'Why didn't we buy more chairs?'"

Before the service, Fred's widow, Cindy, and their two daughters, Alysia and Cassidy, spoke to newspaper reporter Dan Brannan. Cindy said, "[Don Piper] wasn't surprised about our divine appointment and had an understanding that God is at work in our world and in our individual lives to reach out to us and reveal himself to us." She went on to say, "I felt a strong connection with [Don], because he brought us reassurance about Fred's complete joy and peace in heaven. This is something we knew, but to hear him express this sentiment in a real way, because he has experienced heaven, was like a warm blanket for our hearts."[1]

I'd like to tell you something I learned about Fred and Cindy. They married when she was eighteen and together they built a successful ministry at the Maryville church. On Saturday night before his death, Fred was home with the family. In Cindy's words, "That night, he and I were goofing off and laughing. In the midst of our joking around, he looked at me and said, 'You know, you are my best friend.'"

She smiled and they continued their bantering. But after his death, she said, "That is now a very precious moment to me. In the goofiness of the moment for him to have stopped and said those words is a gift from God. God knew I would need that."

Six weeks had passed before I spoke at the church, and she was still grieving her loss. She talked openly about Fred, whom she had known since she was fourteen years old. "I have a huge hole in my heart with him no longer here. There are moments I think about living the rest of my life without that connection. It's painful to think about that. I was looking forward to spending the rest of my life with somebody and the next day I don't have him anymore."

On the Sunday evening of the day Fred died, grief-stricken Cindy picked up *90 Minutes in Heaven*. Her husband had read the book two years earlier when he first contacted me. Several times he had mentioned the book to her, but she hadn't read it.

That night she read the first three chapters. "Chapters two and three brought me so much comfort and understanding," Cindy said. "I don't know how I would have made it through that night without knowing what Fred was experiencing in heaven."

She gave copies of my book to the police, firefighters, and emergency-room staff who had been involved that night. She invited all of them to First Baptist Church, and hundreds came in uniform the night I spoke.

Cindy had insisted that I still come to speak at the church. I'm so glad she did. She told me that she still reflects on the love and friendship she and Fred shared. She frequently quotes Romans 8:28, "And we know that in all things God works for the good to those who love him, who have been called according to his purpose" (NIV).

"That verse conveys Fred's perspective on life. No matter what happens, we can allow God to bring good out of this, even if it is evil," Cindy said. "That is what Fred would want us to do. I pray for the man who shot Fred and pray that he will find peace from God."

I also want to mention the results from the life and death of Fred Winters. Cindy and those at the church have received boxes of cards and letters. Mark Jones told me about an email from a college student, saying that, "The student from Alabama says he is praying for us every day." He reflected that this young man is probably around twenty, working on his degree with huge decisions ahead, and yet he is thinking of someone else.

One church compiled a message tribute called "You Are Not Alone," which let those at First Baptist in Maryville know they were standing by them and praying for them.

They've received messages from around the world; many of which weren't in English. The word spread and many people expressed their compassion. Most of them had the consistent theme that they were praying for Fred's family and the congregation.

Mark also said, "There's something encouraging and comforting in knowing that God has prompted Christians we'll probably never meet to pray for people in the middle of a cornfield in Illinois. We believe that those prayers are being offered up on our prayers and they are tremendously impacting our church in a positive way."

After I had been to the church, they posted these interesting facts on their website: the Sunday after my visit, 1,483 people attended church services. In the weeks after Fred's death, the church witnessed an increase of 278 people at Sunday services. Between March 8 and May 17, average church attendance grew by 210 people in the morning and 230 in the evening service, and morning Sunday school classes increased by 80. On Easter Sunday, 36 people professed faith in Jesus Christ and joined the church.

As I've reflected on that tragedy, I admit I don't understand—and no one does. But I believe God used Fred Winters not only in his life, but in his death to provide a powerful legacy and a greater reward in heaven.

Letters from the Gulf

Not long after *90 Minutes* came out, I started hearing from military personnel serving in Iraq and Afghanistan, as well as their family members. By early January 2010, I had received 687 such emails. Their stories of faith, sacrifice, and loss touched me. I was moved that God would use my simple message to change their lives.

Here are a few samples.

I'm a National Guard soldier from the state of Alabama. My unit and I are currently on deployment in Iraq. We have been away from home since the summer of 2006. I got the chance to go home for two weeks in early March of last year. While at home, my wife introduced me to your book. I have been a Christian for years, and my wife is also a follower of Christ.

She told me how good your book was, so I
decided to pick it up at a bookstore. After returning
to Iraq, I started to read *90 Minutes in Heaven*, and
I must say that this book is an incredible story. I
couldn't put it down.

I wanted to let you know how inspirational your
story is to someone who is already a believer. It
gave me great reassurance about heaven. Not to say
I didn't already believe how wonderful it will be,
but your book bolstered my willingness to get there
someday and sit with the Father.

I can't possibly imagine what pain you must have
gone through, both physical and mental, or what
strain that must have put on your family. What you
did, to keep fighting to stay alive, and to be able to
share this incredible story takes more guts than I
could ever have.

Through reading your book, I know God has
a plan for you and your life and ministry. I'm glad

you're alive today to tell your story. I want to let you know how inspirational your story has been to me, and that it has strengthened my faith. I know that one day I will go to the great heaven where you went.

Thank you for sharing your story so that people like me can be inspired to become better Christians.

Over here in the army, we face many temptations to sin, but your story has strengthened my willingness to live harder for God, to do whatever I can to praise him, and share not only his story, but also yours. Sometimes it takes miracles to get people to believe.

I'm sure the miracle you experienced will influence many to come to know Christ. You have done so much, and I wanted to thank you for it.

⚬⚬⚬

I wanted to thank you for writing your inspirational book. Our son died in Iraq, in October 2005, while serving with the Marine Corps. We are Christians and through prayer and the love and support of so many, we've been able to accept his death and know that he's safe and happy in heaven.

Throughout this journey, I often wondered if I had faith enough to get me through the sorrow and I often asked why.

We saw God's work through the life of our son, and his death has led us to educate youth in the price of freedom. We have established a memorial fund to send students to Arlington Cemetery each year. The response from those trips has been remarkable. God is great and I found deep comfort in reading your book. Thank you and God bless you for your work.
—Nancy Szwydek, Warfordsburg, PA

———∞———

I wanted to write and thank you for putting your experience into words in *90 Minutes in Heaven*.

My only child was killed in Iraq in March. He was only twenty-five. I was a single mother. When I found myself pregnant and unmarried, I thought my family would disown me. I should have known better because they're devout Christians (my mom's dad was a Baptist minister).

They didn't disown me, and I came to realize very quickly that my son was God's gift to me. Having that child turned my life around. He was the light of my life.

Since my son's death I have had many people tell me how strong I am. I've explained that I know God has a plan in this; because I don't understand the plan doesn't mean it doesn't exist.

Even though I know better, at night when it's quiet I've found myself questioning a lot of things. For example, I've questioned the existence of heaven. What if it's something we humans say exists to make the hurts in this world go away? What if when we die, that's all there is? Maybe I should have been ashamed to think that way, but the pain and the grief took over my thoughts.

Last week, I finally went to the bookstore. I'm not the only mother who ever lost her child and I figured that maybe I needed to get some self-help book to guide me through the journey. As I looked at the books in the self-help section, I didn't feel compelled to purchase any of them. Then I went to the religious section and found *90 Minutes in Heaven*.

Last night, I read it straight through. Thank you so much because I needed that message. I needed to believe that one day I would see my baby again. I'll see him whole and he'll be singing and welcoming me and I'll once again feel his hugs. My journey through this isn't over, but I'm deeply indebted to you for putting *your journey* into words.

My son died in Iraq in the summer of 2005.

The week of his funeral I saw your book *90 Minutes in Heaven*. I read the first part of it while I was still inside the store. I didn't buy it: I was probably still in shock.

I don't remember much about that day, but I remembered the title and I wanted to read it when I was ready. Two months later, I bought the book and read it in its entirety. It comforted me as I continued to struggle with the loss of a great son. I wondered what he was experiencing.

My son and I had a special talk before he left. He was a Christian and possibly the best and bravest person I've ever known. He knew he might die but said, "If we don't fight the terrorists over there we'll be fighting them here at home."

Perhaps you can understand why I read the book again a month ago and then passed it to a woman who struggled with her own loss. She has since told me that it helped her.

Today I was in an airport and found your new book, *Daily Devotions Inspired by 90 Minutes in Heaven*. The story of the soldier who died in Iraq touched me: someone read *90 Minutes in Heaven* to him as he lay dying.

I read that story just before I watched several military members getting ready to board a plane for who knows where. My husband is an officer in the Ohio National Guard. He had returned from Afghanistan just before my son left for Iraq.

God has given you a special ministry. There are many grieving people in this world, and at this time, many new Gold Star families (those who have lost someone serving in the military). At times, the grief is overwhelming. We went from having a happy, healthy son to being lost without him. It's a comfort to know that this life is only temporary and eternal life with our Savior (and my son) is coming.

I had to write you. This week I finished reading *90 Minutes in Heaven*. I know you've heard this again and again, but I have to thank you from the bottom of my heart for writing the book.

We lost our marine son in Iraq in 2004. He was nineteen years old. My husband and I are believers.

Deep down I've known our son is in a better place. Despite that, I still continued to wonder if he is truly happy now.

The day our son left home before being deployed to Iraq, he and I were in the kitchen. He looked at me and said, "I worry about you and Dad and how you'll be if something happens to me."

I hugged him and said, "Don't worry about us; we'll be fine. You take care of yourself and come home." Whenever we heard from him while he was in Iraq, he wanted to make sure we were all right. He would tell us he was praying for us. Imagine that! He was the one in danger, but he thought of us.

Because of his attitude and concern, I wondered if he was sad because we had to endure this tragedy. After reading your description of heaven, I'm convinced he is now happy and enjoying eternity in the presence of God and everyone that knew and loved him.

I have bought and been given numerous books on death and mourning, and everything that goes along with losing a child. I've never been able to finish a single one. I started them but couldn't continue with them because they made me too sad. *Your book is the first book I have finished* and I couldn't put it down. I wished your description of heaven could have gone on and on.

In the years since we have lost our son, I've met several people who have lost children and have recommended your book to all of them and pray they will find the comfort I did.

Your story is truly heartwarming and inspiring, and I admire you for your strength and courage and, despite all your medical issues, the selfless act of sharing your experience with others. I will be praying for you.

Without the love and grace of God and my promise to Nick that we would be fine, we wouldn't have survived our loss. Thank you from the bottom of my heart for bringing me the peace of knowing Nick is truly happy now.

My name is Bobbie Samme. I read *90 Minutes in Heaven* and *Heaven Is Real*. Every night before bed I read from *Daily Devotions Inspired by 90 Minutes in Heaven*. I'm deeply comforted by your experience and by your words.

My beloved son, Lance Corporal Eric A. Palmisano, USMC, was killed in Iraq on April 2, 2006. He was my youngest son; he was only twenty-seven when he died. He was a brave, excellent Marine and we're proud of him. If you Google Eric A.

Palmisano, you will be able to read all about him and the words of those of us who loved him.

I'm writing to you because the two-year anniversary of Eric's passing over to the other side is this Wednesday, April 2, and after I finished reading *Heaven Is Real* (and rereading *90 Minutes in Heaven*) I felt compelled to write to you.

I know my son is happy and at peace now, but I still miss him very much. He was a loving, attentive son and he brought me many hours of happiness and wonderful memories. I'll reflect on those memories all this week, all the while missing him so badly that my heart aches.

Thank you so much for sharing your story with everyone. Like millions of others, I've found *great* comfort and peace as I mourn the loss of my beloved son, Eric.

May God's peace and strength be with you and allow you to continue your amazing ministry.

—Bobbie Samme, very proud marine mother of Lcpl
Eric A. Palmisano, USMC, KIA Iraq 4.2.06.

I'm sure you've heard it before, but I wanted to let
you know I finished your book, *90 Minutes in Heaven,*
and enjoyed it. My son was killed in Iraq in January
2008, in a house rigged with an IED. Five other
soldiers lost their lives that day.

I've always believed in heaven but as I am sure you
have heard millions of times, I needed reassurance
that my son was all right. He left a wife and two
children.

I hoped he wasn't too sad leaving us all. It helped
that you spoke of having no regrets while you were
in heaven. I know this has all been said to you before
but I felt the need to tell you again: Thank you for
sharing your story.

One Father's Pain

"I had to come to this meeting. My daughter was murdered four weeks ago."

Those first two sentences certainly grabbed my attention.

I had preached a series in a church in Columbia, South Carolina. Afterward, I sat at a table to sign copies of my books.

I like book signings because I get a chance to talk directly with people. And some of them have amazing stories to tell me.

As his words sunk in, I put down my pen and stared at him. "I'm sorry for your loss—"

That's as far as I got before he blurted out his story. Other people waited in line behind him, but I felt that father needed to tell me the full story.

"I went into horrible depression. My heart was broken," he said. "I couldn't accept her death, especially such a violent one." He wiped tears from his

153

eyes before he continued. "I hardly ate anything. I lost weight. I couldn't sleep. As soon as I closed my eyes, my grief overwhelmed me. It didn't get better and my depression grew worse. Friends from my church insisted that I go to our family doctor. I resisted, but they came to my house and took me anyway."

His voice softened, and I leaned forward to hear the rest of his story.

"The doctor said I needed regular meals, rest, and recuperation. But I knew that much. He told me to take better care of myself, or I would die too. I told him I didn't care. But then he said, 'Yes, but your brothers and sisters from church do. They don't want another funeral!' And he phoned in a prescription for a tranquilizer and an appetite stimulant."

"And those helped?"

He held up his hand because he wanted to finish his story. "Right after that, my friends took me to the CVS pharmacy near our home to pick them up."

He told me he stood in line at the pharmacy, but he felt so weak from loss of sleep and little food, he became lightheaded and dizzy. "I felt myself starting to faint. Next to me was one of those bookracks and I grabbed it to break my fall.

"That was enough to brace me. In doing that, somehow I wrapped my hand around one of the books in the rack." He smiled and said that as he stood up he looked at the title of the book he had grabbed.

"It was *90 Minutes in Heaven*. And the word *heaven* seemed to jump out at me. I skimmed through the book and saw the chapter called 'New Normal' and I had to read it. I didn't care about the prescriptions or anything around me."

I smiled at him as he said, "I knew that was a divine appointment."

He held up his obviously well-read copy and asked me to sign it. As I wrote in it, he said, "Isn't God good? I went to the pharmacy to get a prescription to help me, and God put one right in front of my eyes."

I said, "Yes, God is good all the time!"

"I know where my daughter is right now. I can celebrate her life and have a meaningful life myself until God calls me home to be with her."

My Favorite Bible Verses and Quotations

My Favorite Bible Verses about Prayer

> But I would seek God's help
>   and present my case to him.
> He does great things that we cannot
>   understand
>   and miracles that we cannot count.
>
> Job 5:8–9 GW

> It would be unthinkable for me to sin against
> the Lord by failing to pray for you. I will go on
> teaching you the way that is good and right.
>
> 1 Samuel 12:23 GW

Know that the LORD singles out godly
people for himself.
The LORD hears me when I call to him.

Psalm 4:3 GW

Before they call, I will answer.
While they're still speaking, I will hear.

Isaiah 65:24 GW

When you pray, don't ramble like heathens
who think they'll be heard if they talk a lot.
Don't be like them. Your Father knows what
you need before you ask him.

Matthew 6:7–8 GW

At the same time the Spirit also helps us in our
weakness, because we don't know how to pray
for what we need. But the Spirit intercedes
along with our groans that cannot be expressed
in words. The one who searches our hearts
knows what the Spirit has in mind. The Spirit
intercedes for God's people the way God wants
him to.

Romans 8:26–27 GW

I will do anything you ask the Father in my name so that the Father will be given glory because of the Son. If you ask me to do something, I will do it.

John 14:13–14 GW

If any of you needs wisdom to know what you should do, you should ask God, and he will give it to you. God is generous to everyone and doesn't find fault with them. When you ask for something, don't have any doubts. A person who has doubts is like a wave that is blown by the wind and tossed by the sea. A person who has doubts shouldn't expect to receive anything from the Lord. A person who has doubts is thinking about two different things at the same time and can't make up his mind about anything.

James 1:5–8 GW

Never stop praying. Whatever happens, give thanks, because it is God's will in Christ Jesus that you do this.

1 Thessalonians 5:17–18 GW

My Favorite Quotations about Prayer

Don't pray for tasks equal to your pow-
ers; pray for power equal to your tasks.
—Phillips Brooks

Whatsoever we beg of God, let us also work for
it. —Jeremy Taylor

Is your prayer a monologue or a conversation?
—Anonymous

Pray for a tough hide and a tender heart.
—Ruth Graham

Go to prayer and listen. —J. C. Macaulay

Practical prayer is harder on the soles of
your shoes than the knees of your trousers.
—Austin O'Malley

Pray to God, but continue to row to the shore.
—Unknown

Prayer, among sane people, has never superseded practical efforts to secure the desired results. —Santayana

The man who says his prayers at night is a captain posting his sentinels. He can sleep. —Baudelaire

Don't pray when it rains if you don't pray when the sun shines. —Satchel Paige

My Favorite Bible Verses about Comfort

Even if my father and mother abandon
    me,
the Lord will take care of me. . . .
Wait with hope for the Lord.
Be strong, and let your heart be
    courageous.
Yes, wait with hope for the Lord.

Psalm 27:10, 14 GW

When he falls, he will not be thrown
    down headfirst
because the LORD holds on to his hand.

Psalm 37:24 GW

The victory for righteous people comes
    from the LORD.
He is their fortress in times of trouble.

Psalm 37:39 GW

God is our refuge and strength,
    an ever-present help in times of
        trouble.
That is why we are not afraid
    even when the earth quakes
    or the mountains topple into the
        depths of the sea.
Water roars and foams,
    and mountains shake at the surging
        waves.

Psalm 46:1–3 GW

Sing with joy, you heavens!
Rejoice, you earth!

Break into shouts of joy, you mountains!
The LORD has comforted his people
and will have compassion on his
humble people.

Isaiah 49:13 GW

I will ask the Father, and he will give you another
helper who will be with you forever. . . . I will not
leave you all alone. I will come back to you.

John 14:16, 18 GW

Good will and peace from God our Father and
the Lord Jesus Christ are yours! I always thank
God for you because Christ Jesus has shown
you God's good will.

1 Corinthians 1:3–4 GW

We always thank God for all of you as we remember you in our prayers. In the presence of
our God and Father, we never forget that your
faith is active, your love is working hard, and
your confidence in our Lord Jesus Christ is
enduring.

1 Thessalonians 1:2–3 GW

Brothers and sisters, we don't want you to be ignorant about those who have died. We don't want you to grieve like other people who have no hope. We believe that Jesus died and came back to life. We also believe that, through Jesus, God will bring back those who have died. They will come back with Jesus. We are telling you what the Lord taught. We who are still alive when the Lord comes will not go into his kingdom ahead of those who have already died. The Lord will come from heaven with a command, with the voice of the archangel, and with the trumpet call of God. First, the dead who believed in Christ will come back to life. Then, together with them, we who are still alive will be taken in the clouds to meet the Lord in the air. In this way we will always be with the Lord.

1 Thessalonians 4:13–17 GW

We understand what love is when we realize that Christ gave his life for us. That means we must give our lives for other believers. Now, suppose a person has enough to live on and notices another believer in need. How

can God's love be in that person if he doesn't
bother to help the other believer?

1 John 3:16–17 GW

He will wipe every tear from their eyes. There
won't be any more death. There won't be any
grief, crying, or pain, because the first things
have disappeared.

Revelation 21:4 GW

My Favorite Quotations about Comfort

The dew of compassion is a tear. —Lord Byron

It takes a true believer to be compassionate. No
greater burden can be borne by an individual
than to know that no one cares or understands.
—Arthur Stainback

Biblical orthodoxy without compassion is
surely the ugliest thing in the world.
—Francis Schaeffer

Christianity demands a level of caring that transcends human inclination. —Erwin Lutzer

Ten rules for overcoming the blues: Go out and do something for someone else and repeat it nine times. —Anonymous

Job responds (to the destruction of his family and wealth), even before his health and wealth are restored by saying, "All of this is too wonderful for me." Job found contentment and even joy, outside the context of comfort, health and stability. He understood the story was not about him, and he cared more about the story than he did about himself. —Donald Miller[1]

My Favorite Bible Verses about Heaven

The heavens declare the glory of God,
and the sky displays what his hands have
made.

Psalm 19:1 GW

Turn to God and change the way you think and act, because the kingdom of heaven is near.

Matthew 3:2 GW

I give them eternal life. They will never be lost, and no one will tear them away from me.

John 10:28 GW

In our present tent-like existence we sigh, since we long to put on the house we will have in heaven.

2 Corinthians 5:2 GW

We, however, are citizens of heaven. We look forward to the Lord Jesus Christ coming from heaven as our Savior. Through his power to bring everything under his authority, he will change our humble bodies and make them like his glorified body.

Philippians 3:20–21 GW

There will no longer be any curse. The throne of God and the lamb will be in the city. His servants will worship him and see his face. His

name will be on their foreheads. There will
be no more night, and they will not need any
light from lamps or the sun because the Lord
God will shine on them. They will rule as kings
forever and ever.

Revelation 22:3–5 GW

My Favorite Quotations about Heaven

Can you tell a plain man the road to heaven?
Certainly, turn at once to the right, then go
straight forward. —William Wilberforce

Everybody wants to go to heaven, but nobody
wants to die. —Joe Louis (When the Piper
family visited Arlington National Cemetery,
among many famous folks' burial plots we saw
former heavyweight boxing champion and U.S.
Army veteran Joe Louis's grave. I remember
seeing this favorite quote of mine when we
passed his grave.)

Has the world been so kind that you should
leave the world with regret? There are better

things ahead than any we leave behind.
—C. S. Lewis

Heaven goes by favor; if we went by merit, you
would stay out and your dog would go. —Mark
Twain/Samuel L. Clemens (A distant relative
of mine. My grandmother's maiden name was
Clemons, and she was from a town near the
Mississippi River.)

Heaven is a prepared place for prepared people.
—Dwight L. Moody

Notes

Chapter 4

1. Commonly called "Jaws of Life," this is a brand of tools trademarked by the Hurst Jaws of Life Company. The term refers to several types of piston-rod hydraulic tools known as cutters, spreaders, and rams that are used to pry trapped victims from crashed vehicles.

2. "What a Friend We Have in Jesus," words by Joseph Scriven, 1855.

Chapter 5

1. Pim van Lommel, Ruud van Wees, Vincent Meyers, Ingrid Elffench, "Near-death Experience in Survivors of Cardiac Arrest: A Prospective Study in the Netherlands," *Lancet* 358, no. 9298 (December 15, 2001): 2039–45.

A Final Word

1. See 1 Peter 1:8.

Stories of Encouragement

1. Dan Brannan, "Author brings comfort to church struck by tragedy," *The Telegraph* (May 1, 2009), http://www.thetelegraph.com/news/piper-26313-church-winters.html.

My Favorite Bible Verses and Quotations

1. Donald Miller, *A Million Miles in a Thousand Years* (Thomas Nelson, 2009), 197.

Don Piper has been an ordained minister since 1985 and has served in several capacities on church staffs, including six years as a senior pastor. He and his wife, Eva, are residents of Pasadena, Texas, and are the parents of three grown children. Don has appeared on numerous Christian and secular television and radio programs and has been the subject of countless newspaper and magazine features. Every week you will find him preaching and leading conferences and retreats all over the United States and abroad. Don can be contacted at donpiperministries@yahoo.com.

Cecil Murphey has written or coauthored more than one hundred books, including *Gifted Hands: The Ben Carson Story* with Dr. Ben Carson. Cecil can be contacted at www.cecilmurphey.com.

An ideal gift of
comfort and hope

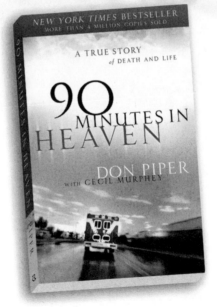

NEW YORK TIMES BESTSELLER
MORE THAN 4 MILLION COPIES SOLD

A TRUE STORY
of DEATH AND LIFE

90 MINUTES IN HEAVEN

DON PIPER
WITH CECIL MURPHEY

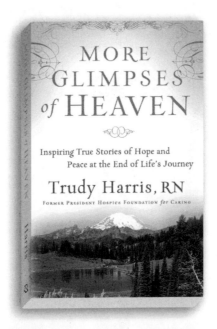